THE
TOKEN
WOMAN

A GUIDE TO THRIVING AS A
FEMALE LEADER IN SALES

CHERYL STOOKES

FriesenPress

Suite 300 - 990 Fort St.
Victoria, BC V8V 3K2
Canada

www.friesenpress.com

Copyright © 2020 by Cheryl Stookes
First Edition — 2020

All rights reserved.

No part of this publication may be reproduced in any form, or by any means, electronic or mechanical, including photocopying, recording, or any information browsing, storage, or retrieval system, without permission in writing from FriesenPress.

ISBN
978-1-5255-8680-4 (Hardcover)
978-1-5255-8679-8 (Paperback)
978-1-5255-8681-1 (eBook)

1. BUSINESS & ECONOMICS, LEADERSHIP

Distributed to the trade by The Ingram Book Company

CONTENTS

Introduction	vii
1: Your Resting Bitch Face Need Not Be Career Limiting	1
2: Recognition is Free. Spend Generously	7
3: When You Spot a Unicorn, Create a Unicorn Village	11
4: Hire Carefully. Fire Respectfully	17
5: Speak Slowly and Use Small Words	21
6: The Steady Hand on the Wheel	25
7: The Elephant in the Room Takes Up a Lot of Space	33
8: Keep It Simple, Sister	39
9: On the Road Again	45
10: Super Solvers, Unite!	49
11: 499 Jobs	53
12: Know What? 'Bitches Get Stuff Done'	57
Endnote: Unfinished Business	61

DEDICATION

For past, present and future Unicorns

INTRODUCTION

The growing pile of unread business books in my home office gives me anxiety. I walk by them often, pretending not to notice their perfect, unopened covers. I feel a strange combination of pressure and uneasiness knowing they are just sitting there, waiting for me to have enough time to get to them. They all look so daunting.

We all have important stuff to do – and not enough time to do it. My goal in writing this book was to cut to the chase and provide practical, helpful tips on becoming an effective sales leader, in a straightforward and approachable way. As you read, I hope you learn a few things to help you navigate this crazy profession called sales, and occasionally laugh out loud.

The lessons presented here are shared through my experiences of hiring, developing and leading salespeople for more than 15 years. You will see the good, the bad, and the ugly tears (see Chapter 7). My aim is to help more women become kick-ass, successful sales leaders. Trust me, the corporate world needs many more of them!

If you are a woman in sales leadership, or aspire to be, I hope this short how-to is helpful in your career journey.

1

YOUR RESTING BITCH FACE NEED NOT BE CAREER LIMITING

Becoming a technology sales leader was not my life's master plan.

Throughout my school years I was determined to be a lawyer. My husband Trevor says it is because I take pleasure in being right. I told my family it was what I wanted to do and majored in Political Studies at university, a common path before going to law school. After my second year at Queen's University in Kingston, Ontario, I wrote the Law School Admission Test and fully intended to apply.

My third year as an undergrad changed everything. I was a visiting student at the University of Edinburgh in Scotland. Our schools were sister universities and together with 17 fellow Queen's students, I participated in an exchange program for the year. It was an incredible deal because we did not have to pay any additional tuition and I thought it would be an exciting opportunity. I was right, and my year in Scotland was life altering.

I wanted to visit more of the United Kingdom and Europe while I was living there, so I picked up a bartending job at a pub on Edinburgh's famous Royal Mile to fund my travel. The pub was more than 100 years old, with vintage 1960s décor and occasional live folk music and poetry readings. The same locals came in every night. We had three beers on tap and a small handful of spirits; that was it. The regular customers were fantastic characters and we engaged in spirited banter. They enjoyed the novelty of my Canadian accent.

That year I played on a co-ed varsity korfball team, which sounds made up but is an actual sport. Think of it as a combination of basketball and European handball, with four female players and four male players on each team. Our team travelled extensively for tournaments throughout England and Wales, allowing me to see a lot of the U.K. on a shoestring budget. The travel was not high-end – we rented a minibus and slept on the floors of the hosting team members' flats. Each tournament ended with a big "fancy dress" celebration on the Saturday night that was basically a boozy costume party.

Mid-way through the year abroad, I began to rethink law as a career path. I have a lot of respect for lawyers and believe theirs is a noble profession, but I started to question whether it was right for me. Upon returning to Canada for my final year at Queen's, I started considering a few different career paths that were directly related to my degree – government, academia, and something called political risk management that sounded important but I'm still not sure what it means. None of these options was particularly inspiring to me.

I decided to take a different approach. Rather than think about what I *should* be doing, I thought about what I *loved* to do and was passionate about. Two things came to mind: sports and improvisational comedy. I had competed in sports all my life and enjoyed playing pretty much any game I could win. My other passion, improv, was one of my favorite activities from my school years. In both high school and university, I was a member of an improvisational comedy troupe. In high school we performed at assemblies and competitions across the school district. In university we performed in dive bars in Kingston, Ontario.

I wondered if I could somehow combine these two things and get paid for it. Turns out there is no such thing as improv baseball. However, there was a path I could take that would allow me to combine my passion for competition with a love of performing: a career in sales. I signed up for an open-house-style interview with a technology company in Toronto that was hiring new grads for entry-level sales positions and knew the moment I walked in that I was in the right place.

After graduation, I began my career selling information technology products and services to customers, primarily over the phone. Every day was a competition – who made the most calls, who placed the most orders, who had the highest sales; it was the best! I did not have a technology background, but the company that hired me had an excellent training program and a leadership team that took the time to teach me how to leverage all the resources available to help.

At first, it was overwhelming. Those first few weeks, I went home every night and worried that I had made a big mistake and was in way over my head. I had studied politics at school and now I was drinking from a firehose of information from hundreds of different original equipment manufacturers (OEMs) and learning dozens of complex licensing scenarios. What the hell was I thinking? I feared I had made a huge error and began thinking about Plan B career paths.

Around the three-month mark, things began to click and I felt like I was hitting my stride. I was promoted from an inside sales rep to an account manager's role where I had my own customers and quota. I did not consider myself a gifted seller by any stretch of the imagination. But I worked hard and prided myself on providing excellent customer support and being very responsive to my clients. If I did not know the answer to a question, I was always honest about it and committed to finding the answer. I got back to my customers in a timely way and always followed through on my commitments. By focusing on providing exemplary customer support, I earned the right to compete on many opportunities within my customer base and won more than I lost. My early career was an exciting time and I look back on it with fond memories.

Halfway through my second year in sales, my boss was promoted and I was tapped on the shoulder to take over leading the team. While thrilled at the opportunity, I secretly felt like a fraud and was terrified someone would catch on that I had no idea what I was doing as a manager. I was also extremely nervous about moving from being a peer to my teammates to suddenly becoming their boss. Many of the staff on my team were much older than I, with more experience in sales.

I accepted the position and approached it in the only way I knew how: by pretending I knew what I was doing and putting on the bravest face I could muster. "I've got this!" my look of determination would tell people, as I walked through the hallways. "I am totally confident!" my furrowed brow would say, as I listened intently in meetings. Portraying an image of a focused leader would become my thing and people would take me seriously. I was no longer a seller; I was a manager now and people would respect me.

And then it happened. I was sitting in a one-on-one meeting with my director. We had just reviewed the sales forecast numbers and began wrapping up when she said six words that terrified me: "Can I offer you some feedback?" My stomach dropped and my heart started to race. My mind was going in a million directions and I began thinking about every possible doomsday scenario that would happen next. "Absolutely!" I chirped, at a much higher volume than intended.

I sat back down, casually trying not to lose my lunch on her desk, and braced myself. She continued: "I have been fortunate to get to know you pretty well and interact with you on a one-on-one basis. I see your warmth and the passion you have for your team. *However*, a lot of people at the company don't know you like I do, and they find you intimidating and unapproachable." My heart sank and I wanted to crawl into a hole. I said something awkward like "Okey-dokey," and promptly left.

I vividly recall the next 24 hours. I was furious at my manager. "How dare she say that to me? She is so wrong. I am a very nice and approachable person, and everyone wants to talk to me, dammit!" I would say these things mainly to my oversized chocolate Labrador, who thought I was a lunatic.

On day two of my pity party, it hit me. My boss had done something special for me by taking the time to share that information. She was giving me the gift of feedback. From then on, my perspective changed. In sharing that insight, my boss demonstrated that she cared and wanted me to succeed at the company. She was concerned about how others were perceiving me and how that might affect my progression. She wanted others to see what *she* saw.

I went into her office at the end of that day and thanked her for having the professional respect to give me that feedback. We sat down for a few minutes and she offered some tips on how I could help change others' perceptions. We decided one strategy would be for me to take "floor walks" every morning around the sales floor, to talk with people I didn't know very well. "I can do that," I thought. "I love talking to people." And as a bonus, I had my secret weapon: the chocolate Lab.

At the time, I worked in a dog-friendly environment. Dogs in the office were a regular thing and I often brought mine with me to work. He mostly hung out in my office, wagged his tail and freely passed gas. Nothing wraps up a meeting quite as fast as a 120-pound Labrador letting one go in a confined space.

Each morning, I carved out 15 minutes for the two of us to do the rounds on the sales floor. I walked up and down the rows, chatting with different sellers while my dog enjoyed an abundance of ear scratches. Some of the sales reps started buying treats for the morning visits and my Lab would snack his way through the rows. The sellers began to see me in a different light. I chatted with them casually, we joked about whatever goofy thing my dog had done the night before, and we bonded over their own pet stories. I made mental notes of the pictures and decorations on people's desks. By simply walking the floor, I learned so much about the people with whom I worked.

It was amazing how much my relationships evolved within the organization over the coming months. People from across the company would come into my office for a quick chat or to seek advice. A lot of these people were not even on my team; they just perceived me as a normal person and not the scary lady who looked angry all the time. Or maybe they just really liked my dog.

A couple of key lessons stuck with me from this time. The first is that feedback is a gift. If someone offers you feedback, thank them. It might not be easy to hear, and at times you might disagree, but appreciate that the person has taken the time to give it to you. I am grateful that my manager took the time to provide me with that gift. Over the course of my career I have offered the same gift of feedback to my direct reports, peers, managers and friends. In return, they have done the same for me.

The other important lesson is that while you do not need to be friends with all your co-workers, especially when they report to you, being *friendly* goes a long way. And it is okay to bring your personality into your work. I have a wide variety of interests. I am a huge sports fan, particularly baseball and basketball. I enjoy improv comedy. I love karaoke bars, the stranger the better. I can juggle. These quirky things have made their way into my work life over the years – whether playing on the company softball team, hosting a partner event at The Second City Comedy Club, singing in a karaoke fundraiser, or even juggling to celebrate a large sales deal. These things gave me joy, but they also made my co-workers happy. By bringing more of myself and my personality to work, it gave others permission to do the same.

My intensity could have become an inhibitor to my career progression. Instead it became an unexpected blessing that changed the trajectory of my early career. And all because I embraced a gift that was given to me. Feedback: 1; Resting Bitch Face: 0.

2

RECOGNITION IS FREE. SPEND GENEROUSLY

Early in my career I worked for a charismatic sales director. He radiated positivity and his energy was infectious. Month-end was always a big deal for our company. We adopted an all-hands-on-deck attitude, ordered in food and snacks for the sales teams, and almost everyone stayed late to focus on closing final deals. It was always my favorite day of the month! I needed more hobbies.

During one month-end, I noticed my boss sitting in his office, studying a list of names and sales figures. He had shut down his computer and was reading the list over and over, clearly focusing on memorizing it. After an hour or so, he left the list behind and walked around the sales floor. One by one, he approached every seller who had hit quota that month, addressed them by their first name and shook their hand while offering congratulations. He cited the specific details. "Congrats, Mike, on finishing at 159% of plan this month; great work!" "Congrats, Angela, for finishing at 104% and hitting plan in your very first month in this role." It was inspiring to watch the pride on my co-workers' faces. The sales teams appreciated that he took the time to recognize their work and were gratified that he had learned their names and details about their client business.

Every month the director's routine was the same. The sellers that hit plan got excited because they knew they were going to get a personal handshake and congratulations from the boss. It became a point of motivation for them to overachieve and it had a very positive impact on the company's culture. The entire exercise of reviewing the names and sales figures, memorizing them and walking around the sales floor to give out personal recognition took less than three hours a month – yet it meant so much to so many people. The sales director invested the time to provide recognition and it paid exponential dividends.

In 2018 I took on a role leading North American partnerships and marketing for a technology solution provider. I loved the position and referred to it as my dream job. Most of my previous experience had been in sales leadership, and I was suddenly thrust into a new world of partner programs, customer marketing and corporate events. One of the best parts of the job was hiring a group of new managers and building new departments within the organization. It was uncharted territory for all of us, and we were in it together.

When I was promoted to my next role a year later, I received a thank-you note from one of the more tenured managers on the team. She said I was the first person she ever reported to that had invited her to join important meetings with the senior executive team and encouraged her to present her ideas. This surprised me. She had been with the company for five years and had been a manager for two of them. She was bright and had excellent communication and presentation skills. Why hadn't she been given that opportunity before?

Recognition of employees is free. It literally costs nothing to tell someone they are doing a great job or provide them with an opportunity to shine in front of others. And yet, every one of her previous managers had failed to give her that chance. What a missed opportunity!

In any job, and particularly in sales, there are good months and bad months. One manager I know described a career in sales as being a hero on the 30th of every month and a loser on the 1st. He was not fun at parties, but he was not wrong. Being a brand-new seller in a new territory is especially hard. It requires hearing the word "no" from customers, dozens if not hundreds of times before hearing the word "yes." It can be very discouraging.

Most sales companies do a decent job of celebrating top performances. They host monthly company-wide calls and annual sales conferences to recognize the top 10 percent of the salesforce. These things are important, and they are common in the technology industry. The very best companies and leaders set themselves apart by celebrating small wins whenever possible. They take the time to congratulate a salesperson for securing a meeting with a new prospect, executing a well-run sales call, leveraging an effective prospecting technique or winning a first purchase order from a customer, regardless of the revenue.

In 2019 I was tasked with leading a significant multi-year expansion of my company across Canada. This involved hiring dozens of new sellers and managers across the country in the span of a few months. These salespeople were responsible for prospecting in new territories and generating new business from scratch. It was a tough challenge and whenever possible, our leadership team looked for opportunities to recognize and celebrate small wins. We hosted regular team huddles and had sellers lead best-practice sessions on a variety of topics. We would broadly share winning strategies and customer success stories and we made a big deal of someone winning a new account. These gestures went a long way with our growing team and contributed to high employee satisfaction and team camaraderie. The efforts were not time consuming and they did not cost us any money. At the same time, they were invaluable.

3

WHEN YOU SPOT A UNICORN, CREATE A UNICORN VILLAGE

Being a female leader in sales often means being outnumbered by men. When I was first promoted to director in 2012 and walked into my first senior leadership meeting, I looked around the room wondering when the token woman was going to show up. Then I realized she was not coming; she was me. Sadly, for many companies that is still the case in 2020.

In my early days, my go-to move was to try to be one of the guys. Growing up, I considered myself a tomboy and was comfortable holding my own with the boys on the ball diamond or basketball court at school. This translated well in technology sales at a time when I was often the only female leader in a group of men. I had my trusty Bitch Face ready and was never afraid to speak up and offer my opinion.

I had heard horror stories about female executives in the industry who were threatened by other strong women. In their eyes, their role as the alpha female was in jeopardy when another woman entered the picture. I have never understood this school of thought and always believed that a company benefits greatly from increased diversity in leadership roles. As such, I did my best to coach and mentor high-potential female employees, with the intent of helping them accelerate their careers into leadership positions.

As my career progressed, I was encouraged to see more women in my company joining the leadership ranks. While still outnumbered, a growing number of strong females were getting promoted to manager- and director-level roles. This was exciting to me and the dynamic of our leadership meetings began changing for the better. Much more diverse ideas and viewpoints were offered in the meetings, allowing us to accelerate the growth and success of the organization.

In 2013 I was in Austin, Texas at a multi-day leadership meeting. These types of meetings were common for my company. Our leaders from across North America would gather for several days and share new strategies; then we would go home to our branch offices and roll out several new initiatives with our teams. We were always optimistic leaving the meetings, determined that what we were about to initiate would be perfect and convinced that we would have the discipline to stick with the plan long-term. We almost never did, despite our best intentions, with day-to-day pressures taking precedence once we returned to home base.

Near the end of this meeting, one of the newest female managers raised her hand and stood up. "This is my first leadership meeting," she said. "For years, whenever my manager attended these things, he would come back to the office as if he were jacked up on candy. He would run around in circles for a few days like a maniac and eventually he would pass out. Can we not do that?"

I knew right then that this woman was special and I dubbed her The Candy Lady. I tried to get to know her and quickly learned she was bright, talented, as funny as hell, and she did not put up with crap from anyone. At the same time, she was sincere, compassionate and a huge advocate for her team. She was a Unicorn.

Years later, while working for a technology manufacturer in Raleigh, North Carolina, I was selected to participate in a women's leadership development program with 20 high-potential female leaders from across the organization. It was an unforgettable experience and one I am grateful to have been part of. An element of the program included attending a Women's Leadership Conference in Dallas where we heard inspiring presentations from Carla Harris – accomplished Wall Street executive, motivational speaker, gospel singer and author – and Dr. Brené Brown, a renowned research professor on the topics of courage, vulnerability, shame, and empathy. Our leadership cohort included representatives from China, Japan, Brazil, Canada and the United States. English was not the first language of many in the group, so collaborating and communicating effectively with one another took patience and creativity.

On the second day of the conference, Brené's opening keynote focused on courage and vulnerability, setting the tone for the day. She joined our group of 20 in the afternoon breakout segment and I still get goosebumps thinking about how impactful that session was. The afternoon was emotional for many of us. Brené gave us the courage to be vulnerable, and many women in the group shared some of the most personal, touching and in some cases, heartbreaking stories I had ever heard.

When the session wrapped, I was emotionally exhausted. All I wanted to do was go up to my hotel room and order room service and a large glass of wine. I needed to reflect on what I had heard that afternoon and come to grips with the intense feelings of vulnerability I was experiencing. Just as I changed into my hotel robe and prepared to wallow, my phone rang. It was one of my colleagues from the group. She said, "Cheryl, take one hour to have the pity party you need to have, then meet me in the lobby. We are going out."

An hour later, despite every ounce of me wanting to bail, I found myself in the hotel lobby. I was soon joined by the women in the program, who all looked as exhausted as I felt. My Ringleader colleague said today had been a tough day, and we were going to go sing it out; we were going to karaoke. Most of the group looked horrified. I was immediately ecstatic. I absolutely love karaoke bars. To be clear, I am a terrible singer. Think of the scene from *My Best Friend's Wedding* when Cameron Diaz's character, Kimmy, serenades her fiancé terribly off-key but with passion and commitment. That is me. I am a Karaoke Kimmy.

As we approached the bar, I realized that something felt slightly different about the place. We walked in and there she was in all her glory: a drag queen dressed as Cher, the "Cher-e-oke" host that evening. What followed was one of the greatest nights of my career. We 20 female leaders from around the world took over the bar and sang our hearts out. There was an array of Kimmy-like performances that evening: Disney ballads, Running Man contests, singalongs with the bartenders, and duets with Drag Queen Cher. It was ridiculous and incredible. We shut the place down and laughed the entire way back to the hotel.

From then on, Ringleader became someone special to me, both personally and professionally. We spoke regularly and acted as one another's accountability buddies. We called each other on good days and bad days. We coached each other through difficult conversations and celebrated wins together. I admired her immensely and learned so much from her leadership approach. I valued her candor, humor and creativity. She too was a Unicorn.

A few months later, that same group of women travelled to Beijing for the next portion of the leadership program. On the second day at the company's headquarters, Ringleader and I were walking through the lobby of the main campus when suddenly I stopped and could not believe my eyes. There it was: a karaoke booth! I had never seen such a thing and certainly did not expect to find one in the main lobby of the head office of a conservative global technology company. We looked at each other with mutual glee and thought the same thing: we MUST sing.

As we got into the booth and browsed the song list, Ringleader reached into her bag and pulled out two party wigs. I had so many questions. Why did she have wigs? Why would she bring them with her to Beijing? Did she always randomly carry wigs around just in case she stumbled upon a karaoke booth? I was strangely impressed by her forward thinking and preparation. There was only one thing left to do: put on the party wigs, and sing.

A few months later, I decided to rejoin my previous company in Austin where I had met the original Unicorn, The Candy Lady. I was struck by how much she had grown and developed as an executive in the four years I had been away from the company. We collaborated often and celebrated each other's successes. I joined her and a few other colleagues as proud board members of the company's diversity and inclusion group. It organized and hosted various events and forums throughout the year to inspire, empower and encourage collaboration among all employees, and celebrate the diversity of women in technology.

Within a year there was an opening on my team for a senior leader to manage a very strategic part of our business. With no suitable internal candidate, it was a no-brainer who would be perfect for the job; I reached out to the Ringleader from Raleigh to gauge her interest. She joined the company and for the next 18 months, I worked alongside two of the most influential and incredible female leaders I have ever known. We created our very own Unicorn Village! The village was open to both women and men who valued transparency, hard work, honesty and authenticity. We found great pleasure and humor working together and became champions for inclusiveness within the organization. We did our best to elevate high-potential talent across the organization regardless of gender, background or ethnicity. I am a better leader and a better person because of the time I spent in the Unicorn Village working alongside both women. Sadly, I am no better a singer.

4

HIRE CAREFULLY. FIRE RESPECTFULLY

A key part of a sales leader's role is to hire, develop and retain salespeople. Over the course of my career I have hired more than 150 sellers. I have always subscribed to the Marcus Buckingham school of hiring. In his book, *First, Break All the Rules,* he says leaders should always hire employees for their talents, not for their skills or knowledge. Buckingham defines a talent as a recurring feeling, thought or behavior that can be used in an effective way. And it cannot be taught.

When hiring salespeople, I look for three distinct talents. The first is competitiveness. If you are competitive, your desire to win comes from a deep internal need to earn your customers' business and beat your competition. In sales, this is extremely important because there is no shortage of competitors vying for the same clients. The second talent is discipline. Prospecting is hard. Sellers must be very persistent in their efforts and this requires a high degree of self-motivation and daily perseverance. The third talent is empathy, the ability to know what another person is thinking or feeling. If a salesperson can define and articulate a customer's problem in a way that resonates with them, they will be able to help and provide the customer with value.

You will notice I did not include a laundry list of required years of sales experience, specific training or technical certifications. I believe a post-secondary education is critical because it develops key life skills, but it has never mattered to me what someone studied at college or university. I majored in Political Studies and have had a successful career in technology sales. Good salespeople come from a wide variety of disciplines.

Even if your team is at its desired headcount, hiring never stops. Like the general manager of a baseball team, the best leaders are always thinking about drafting the best prospects in the market while simultaneously developing the players on their team.

Every sales team has A, B and C players. The A players, the top 20 percent of the sales force, typically contribute a significant portion of the team's revenue and profit. These are the most valuable people in your sales organization and spending time to develop them pays exponential dividends. I recently watched *The Last Dance*, a 2020 sports documentary miniseries that highlights the career of Michael Jordan and the Chicago Bulls' championship teams of the 1990s – especially the run-up to their sixth National Basketball Association title in eight seasons. It was an excellent reminder that even the best basketball player of all time craved coaching, feedback and development. Everyone needs a coach. Michael Jordan needed Phil Jackson, and your top sellers need you.

The B players, the middle 60 percent, make up most of your team. They are good but not great, or they are great at times but not all the time. Your opportunity as a leader is to identify the high-potential Bs who have the innate talent to become As, and to invest extra time with them to help them improve their ranking. A bonus tip is to pair your high-potential Bs with the A players on your team who have expressed a desire to take on more responsibility. Not only will those Bs learn from the best and raise their game, you are giving your A players a development opportunity while allowing yourself to better scale your time across the rest of the sales team. It is a win for everyone involved.

Your C players, the bottom 20 percent, can be the toughest group to manage. Many managers fall into the trap of spending far too much time with their Cs. There is an opportunity cost in doing this. An over-concentration on C players comes at the expense of investing more time and energy with your As and high-potential Bs.

There are two types of C players. The first category is those who lack the *skill* to be successful – they are not effective in customer meetings, are unorganized, or are not progressing in the role. In some cases, they are simply in the wrong job and their talents do not match well to sales. This can be the toughest situation for a manager to deal with. You might often really *like* these sellers and enjoy their company in the office, but you know in your gut they are not cut out for the position.

The second category of Cs are those who lack the *will* to be successful. They are not trying and/or they have a poor attitude. Often, they simply do not care. This category of sellers can cause real problems for you and your organization. They can be negative and disruptive in meetings and on the sales floor, and they can drain the morale of their colleagues. I once heard a leader describe this category of sellers as "moldy strawberries." If you do not pluck them out of the basket quickly, the mold will spread through the rest of the batch. The best thing you can do when you discover that you have a moldy strawberry on your team is to partner with your human resources department and work to get that person out of the organization in the most efficient way possible.

Letting people go is a necessary part of the job. The first time I ever had to terminate someone's employment, I could not sleep the night before. I genuinely believed I was going to ruin this person's entire career. Seeing how visibly stressed I was, my director gave me some excellent advice. If you keep someone in a role where they are not successful, he said, you are doing them a disservice. The longer you drag it out, the longer it will take them to find something they are good at. And when people are good at their job, they are happy. After that, whenever I had to let someone go, I felt marginally better about it. I am not saying it ever gets easy to terminate someone's employment. If someone tells you it is easy, it's entirely possible they have sociopathic tendencies.

Several years ago, the first person I ever terminated contacted me on Facebook. We chatted for a while and he said that my firing him was the best thing that had ever happened to him. He was miserable in sales and the move prompted him to start along a different career path where he was much happier. He thanked me. It was helpful for me to know that the next time I had to let someone go, there would be some small comfort in recognizing I was giving that person an opportunity to go and be great somewhere else.

5

SPEAK SLOWLY AND USE SMALL WORDS

I am a huge baseball nerd and have been my entire life. Many toddler photos of me show my unruly, curly blond hair protruding from under a Toronto Blue Jays baseball cap. When I turned four I started playing T-ball and eventually graduated to softball, which I played for more than a decade. My first paying job was as a baseball umpire and I loved it.

In addition to playing, I have also always enjoyed watching professional baseball and I am a diehard Toronto Blue Jays fan. Some of my favorite childhood memories are going to games with my family, and watching the Jays almost every summer night on TV, sitting next to my Dad while we chomped on sunflower seeds. Years later, my husband and I became Jays' season ticket holders and we cheered at as many ballgames as we could each year. This was much easier pre-children, but even with young boys we manage to attend a few Jays' games each season.

In 2018 I was in Austin, Texas wrapping up a meeting with my boss. He had known me for over a decade and knew how passionate I was about baseball. We often talked about the Jays. As I was leaving his office, a co-worker was walking in. It was Christmastime and he was wearing a knitted Houston Astros holiday sweater. I told him I really liked his attire and he said thank you. He should have stopped right there.

Instead, he went on to explain that the gentleman featured on his sweater was named José Altuve and he played baseball for the Houston Astros. I froze in place and it is entirely possible that I blacked out for a second. When I did not respond, he continued that the Houston Astros were a Major League Baseball team. I snapped out of my shock at the sound of my boss's laptop lid closing. I looked over as he was swinging around in his chair, wearing a huge grin. To my colleague he said: "Okay, this is awesome. You are literally mansplaining baseball to Cheryl. I am so excited to see how this plays out." We all laughed, and I played the whole thing very coolly. I casually let Captain Astro know I was a huge fan of the game and told him I looked forward to giving him a hard time about this moment for a while. And trust me – I did, and I still do.

I left the office that day in a great mood. For years I had used the term "mansplain" at work in a half-joking fashion. Merriam-Webster defines mansplaining as: "to explain something to a woman in a condescending way that assumes she has no knowledge about the topic." I was pleased that my boss recognized mansplaining happening in real time and called out Captain Astro on it. I felt supported; most importantly, I was excited to have great material to share in the Unicorn Village that afternoon.

While this is a lighthearted example, mansplaining in the office typically happens much more subtly and at times even unconsciously. It often comes in the form of taking an idea or suggestion that was presented by a woman and subsequently offering that same suggestion, using slightly different language. I call this "manstealing" – the most infuriating version of mansplaining.

I worked with a guy who was notorious for manstealing. His immediate response to any idea presented by a woman was to reject the suggestion, only to bring it up later as if it was an original thought. It was a character flaw, and one that was frustrating for his team. I noticed that this pattern kept happening to one of my colleagues. She was a strong and passionate leader and I considered her a fellow Unicorn. Over and over in staff meetings, her ideas kept getting "manstolen" and she was not getting recognition for her work. It was starting to tick me off.

One evening I shared my frustration with my husband Trevor over dinner. And by dinner, I mean a large glass of wine. Trevor is one of the most level-headed and practical individuals in the world. It is one of the many reasons I love and appreciate him. As I was replaying that day's episode of Manstealing Daily, he asked me why I would not try to repeat my colleague's ideas in the meetings and help give her credit. Of course! The answer was amplification.

I was introduced to the concept of amplification during a keynote address by Carla Harris, a brilliant Wall Street investment banker and motivator. It came back to me a few years later when I conducted an interview with Michelle Chiantara, Cisco's Americas marketing vice-president and a respected leader. The concept was simple. Make a concerted effort to give credit, in a public way, to the person who originated the idea. In practical terms it goes like this.

> **Unicorn:** "I believe we should implement idea X."
> (A few minutes later)
> **Manstealer**: "I believe it would be effective if we rolled out X."
> (Exactly the same thing the Unicorn had said moments before)
> **Others**: "Great idea, Manstealer!"
> **Amplifier**: "Thank you, Manstealer, for supporting ***Unicorn's*** brilliant idea! I agree it is fantastic. Nicely done, ***Unicorn.***"

For the next few months I committed to amplifying my co-worker's ideas whenever possible. And guess what? It became infectious! Not only was the amplification reciprocated by my Unicorn colleague for my ideas, but many others on the team – both male and female – began amplifying one another. It became a cultural norm to give credit where credit was due, and it made for much more enjoyable and collaborative sessions.

Amplification is incredibly rewarding. It generates mutual respect and loyalty and provides employees with a positive and collaborative culture. It is not quite as gratifying as the hard time I give Captain Astro about mansplaining baseball to me, but it is a close second.

6

THE STEADY HAND ON THE WHEEL

My older sister Jenn is an angel. A hard worker in a noble nonprofit profession, a dedicated wife and mother and a selfless friend to many, she is one of the kindest people I know. Jenn is also creative and crafty. Whatever the occasion, her house will be as perfectly decorated as one in a designer magazine, with something homemade baking in the oven. It is all very annoying.

Growing up, Jenn was a model daughter for my parents. Polite and respectful, courteous and helpful, she was an absolute dream child. She was the kind of little girl who would go up to her room for hours to quietly rearrange her stuffed animals in an endless series of combinations such as size, color scheme or animal families. Most of the photos of my sister as a toddler are of her playing quietly with dolls or helping my Mom with something in the kitchen. Everyone appears calm and happy, and the surroundings are impeccably organized. My parents likely should have quit while they were ahead.

Two years after Jenn's arrival, my Dad was on the golf course when my mother went into labor with me. Those were the days before cell phones and my father bought a pager to wear in the final few months of my Mom's pregnancy, "just in case." At the time, the only people who wore pagers were either doctors or drug dealers and I always wondered what category my Dad's golfing friends thought he fit into. The pager buzzed while he was on the 15th hole. He "borrowed" someone's golf cart to zoom back to the clubhouse and drove like a bat out of hell to the hospital – making it just in time for my frantic entrance into the world. I had arrived two weeks early, ready to shake things up.

I was a handful from an early age. While my sister was a perfect sleeper, I preferred to use my crib as a trampoline. While she was quiet and tidy, I was loud and a wrecking ball of destruction throughout the house. Jenn and I mostly got along but I took great pleasure in tormenting her. I frequently messed up her room and perfectly organized stuffed animals, drew mustaches on her dolls, and put my finger an inch from her eyeball repeating, "I'm not touching you." I almost always took things too far and did some serious time in toddler time-out in the early '80s. When I was three, I threw a shoe at my sister's head and my parents sent me to my room. I smugly announced that I was "going there anyway" and sashayed up the stairs.

I was hot-headed as a kid and got myself into trouble on the playground at school on a few occasions. In grade four I was playing baseball with the boys at recess and the school bully was taunting me, saying girls could not play baseball and I did not even know how to throw. I responded by nailing him in his left rib cage with a fastball. I suppose that was my first-ever response to being mansplained to; Captain Astro got off easily!

As an adult, my temperature still rises from time to time. My husband Trevor and I have had our share of arguments, usually lasting several hours longer than they logically should have because I would not back down on some trivial point. At work I have gotten myself into some hot water. As a seller I remember disagreeing with my manager on an issue and throwing him under the bus about it in a team meeting. It was not my finest moment, but I later apologized to him and the two of us forged a much stronger relationship over time. Or maybe I scared the hell out of him and he was nice to me out of fear.

Early on in sales leadership I learned that I had a lot of eyes on me and the salespeople on my team took cues from my behavior, both good and bad. If I lost my cool, my employees would do the same, so it was important that I set the right example.

That was and is not always easy. Often, crap is flying at sales leadership from all directions – customer escalations, sellers' mistakes, pressure around metrics and sales quotas – and the occasional urge to fly off the handle is real. I knew, however, that if I wanted to have a successful career as a leader that simply was not an option. The most important thing I could do for myself and my team in times of adversity was to be the steady hand on the wheel.

There are three key strategies I have learned over the years to do this effectively.

1. **The Three Email Rule.** We have all seen it play out. A mistake is made and a salesperson fires off a heated email to a member of the sales support team. Sales support responds, putting the blame right back on that salesperson. A seller replies, with everyone's boss now receiving a copy. Flaming emails are now flying back and forth in all directions and people are upset and frustrated, no closer to a resolution.

   From the beginning, I stressed the importance of working effectively with sales support and made it clear to my team that it was not acceptable for anyone to act disrespectfully toward other departments. Support departments are critical to the success of any sales organization. The reality is that salespeople cannot do their job successfully without effective sales support behind them. Every quote that is created requires manufacturer part numbers and pricing. For every sale made, an invoice must be generated and eventually collected. Having a strong relationship among support teams makes your life as a sales professional much easier. When mistakes happen, working efficiently as a team to focus on the resolution is much more productive than pointing blame.

The three email rule means that if something takes more than three emails to get resolved, it's time to pick up the phone – or if possible, meet face to face. Speaking with someone in person is much more effective in resolving issues than attempting this by email. It is also a good reminder that the person on the other end of the phone is a human being. People tend to be far more cavalier with their words when sitting behind a keyboard than when they are speaking to someone on the phone or they are three feet apart in a conference room.

2. **Assume Positive Intent.** In 2008 I was tasked with building a field sales team for a U.S.-based company expanding into Canada. Up to this point, the company had done business mainly in the United States and had limited knowledge of the Canadian market, customer base and local laws. Much of my job was explaining Canada to Americans, often in the form of self-deprecating humor. One afternoon I spent a great deal of time working through a tax issue with our accounting team. I was getting frustrated. In my eyes, the issue was simple to fix and I was irritated that I was getting so much pushback from headquarters. After three emails I followed Rule #1 and picked up the phone, fully expecting it to become an argument. I quickly learned that the accounting manager was not challenging me because he was trying to be difficult; he was pushing back simply because he did not know the nuances of tax laws in Ontario.

I believe it is human nature to be inherently helpful. If someone asks you a question, do your best to assure the person that you know their query is well intended. Assume that others are genuinely trying to learn and ultimately want to help you – and the company – to be successful. Of course, there are individuals you will encounter over the course of your career who are just jerks. In these cases, do your best to minimize your interactions with them whenever possible. When you do have to engage, be the consummate professional and kill them with kindness; it will drive them crazy.

3. **Understand the Battlefield.** In 2017 I moved to Raleigh, North Carolina to become chief of staff to the North American president of a global technology company. My experience to that point had largely been in sales leadership, and the new role opened my eyes into the realms of finance, supply chain, marketing and operations. The chief of staff role is a tricky one. As a member of the senior leadership team, I served as a trusted counsel to the North American president in a highly facilitative and strategic role. Other times I did a whole lot of PowerPoint charts and assisted the president with presentations to customers, partners and C-level executives in the company. The nature of my role meant that I was in almost every meeting the president was, so I had exposure to many elements of the business from his vantage point. Because of my access, I had to be extremely careful with what I could and could not share with my colleagues.

I often worked alongside many senior executives as the most junior person in the room. This was new territory for me; I was used to overseeing a large team and being the boss. On more than one occasion I could tell that I had irritated an influential senior member of the leadership team by disagreeing with him in meetings. The look in his eyes made it clear he was ready to punt me back over the Canadian border. Realizing quickly that I was navigating politically tricky waters, I knew I needed to adjust my approach.

For the next few months, I learned to pick my battles. If there was a heated issue being discussed where I did not have a strong opinion one way or another, I shut up and stayed out of it. For topics about which I was passionate and had strong opinions, I learned to be smarter, positioning recommendations in a way that did not alienate my colleagues.

One strategy was learning the fine art of the "pre-wire." Pre-wiring means meeting with key influencers on a policy you are hoping to get implemented, well before bringing it up in a broader setting. This allows you to flush out any potential relevant issues and ultimately get the influencer's support. When it is time to present it to a wider group, there is now at least one influential voice in the room who will second the idea. You might often need to meet a key influencer several times to get them on board with your plan; other times, you will need multiple influencers. I imagine this is what working in Congress feels like and it is likely why a chief of staff typically only lasts 12 to 18 months in the role before they either burn themselves out or move on to a new position with wider responsibility. I was fortunate that my path was the latter and am grateful for the time I spent in the role. It was likely the closest thing to earning a working MBA in diplomatic relations without having to pay tuition.

There are times in one's career when even the most skilled diplomats reach their limits. Some people simply cannot be reasoned with using logical arguments and common sense. Other times, zero tolerance is the only acceptable policy. These include cases of bullying, discrimination, sexism or racism. If you encounter this behavior at work and witness it happening to another employee, immediately engage your boss or the human resources department.

For the most part, conflict at work is completely normal and healthy. Some of the greatest advancements companies make are often generated out of a good old-fashioned debate. In any business, things will go wrong, with customers, employees and support staff generating conflict. Mitigating conflict with humility, professionalism and grace is often what separates the most admired leaders from everyone else. Even if deep down inside, all you really want to do is throw a shoe.

7

THE ELEPHANT IN THE ROOM TAKES UP A LOT OF SPACE

In recent years I have become better educated on the benefits of a diverse and inclusive workforce. I came to realize there is great value in getting a variety of opinions and viewpoints and I started to make a concerted effort to seek input from people of different ages, genders and ethnicities. This has become an extremely rewarding part of my career and I have often been asked to represent my company at speaking engagements, both internally and externally.

My growing interest in diversity and inclusion coincided with many changes happening in my personal life. I got married and became a proud mother of two young boys. When both of our sons were born, my husband and I split the parental leave. It was a special time for both of us, and I remember feeling so grateful that my husband got to spend time with our baby boys. I felt joy at seeing what a strong bond they formed as a result.

In early 2018 I was in a leadership meeting when the topic of paternity leave came up. My ears perked up; I was excited to encourage more male employees to take that time off, based on our family's experience. During the meeting, two senior leaders began talking about a male colleague who was on paternity leave. They spoke about him in a derogatory way. The implication was clear; they felt this man was less committed to his job than they were, and they were disappointed that he took the time off. I remember looking at the other women in the meeting. We all shared the same horrified expression and were unable to fix our faces. The wheels began spinning in my head. Would new fathers in the company miss out on precious time at home for fear of it hurting their chances for promotion? Is this what they thought of women when they took maternity leave? If I have more children, will I be perceived to be less committed to my career? It was a terrible feeling and to this day I regret not speaking up about it.

For the following few months, the elephant remained planted firmly in the room. And it took up a lot of space. Talking about parental leave or childcare no longer felt allowed. Mentioning home responsibilities also felt like a taboo. I made a conscious effort to avoid mentioning my children and my family at work. I hated feeling that I no longer had permission to bring my whole self to the office. Eventually I decided enough was enough, and vowed that if I heard comments like that again, I was going to speak up and address the elephant.

Two years later, I had my moment. It was April 2020 and we were in the early days of the COVID-19 global pandemic. Things had escalated quickly across the world, launching us into a terrifying new normal in North America. Our entire office-based workforce shifted to working remotely, virtually overnight. Our kids were sent home from school and suddenly my husband and I became full-time, home-based working parents and childcare providers for two high-energy boys, ages three and five. While we felt extremely fortunate that we still had jobs, we were struggling. The workload essentially doubled for both of us – managing 10- to 12-hour days of meetings, video calls, deadlines and sales quotas while simultaneously playing the role of home school teachers, caretakers, entertainment staff, and referees to what felt like endless fighting matches between the boys. It was exhausting. I felt like a failure in both realms of my life – being a mom and being a boss.

Some days I would be in my home office for 12-plus hours, feeling tremendously guilty that I could not spend quality time with the kids. I would pop out of my office every hour or so to hand the boys a different electronic device, snack #72 of the day, or turn on another movie. Mostly, I would pray that my youngest son would not come crashing into my office like the Kool-Aid Man when I was on a video call. My husband often bore the brunt of the childcare responsibilities and I felt guilty that he was sacrificing his career to prioritize mine. Other days, I was able to take more of a lead with the kids – ensuring they were logged into and participating in their kindergarten Zoom calls (a special kind of hell), helping them with school activities and getting them outside for fresh air. On those days I felt anxious that I was not keeping up with my work obligations. My inbox would pile up and I would compensate by working late in the evening. It was a losing battle and on more than one occasion I found myself ugly crying on the floor of my home office. I was not sleeping or eating properly because of stress. I was not okay.

I knew that many other parents in our company were also struggling to keep up. They were scared, stressed and uncertain about the future. Parents from across the organization began reaching out to me. They knew I was going through the same thing and they trusted my opinion and advice, which I certainly did not feel qualified to give.

During the first few weeks of the pandemic, we had regular senior leadership meetings. We focused on staying connected with one another and designed relevant training for our employees. In tandem, we were creating customer offers to assist our clients in navigating unprecedented times in their businesses. In one of these meetings, one of my colleagues mentioned that he had called a handful of managers that week to "check in" and was pleased to hear how well everyone was handling everything. Overwhelmingly, the people he talked to told him that everything was great and they were doing well. My inner voice screamed "Bullshit." I worried that the people he spoke with were scared to tell the truth.

This was the moment I had been waiting for; this is when I would speak up! I let him know that while I thought we were doing a good job of providing relevant training for our people, I believed we needed to be doing more to help our working parents. They are struggling, I am struggling, and I would like us to try and do more to support working families, I said.

What came next felt like the longest silence of my career. There was dead air on the call, to the point that I checked to see if my phone was on mute and if anyone had heard me. It was in fact on, everyone had heard me very clearly, and no one said a thing. Not even the Unicorns. I felt deflated. I put my neck out there to advocate on behalf of a significant portion of our employee base, and I failed.

A few days later, one of my colleagues called to thank me. He said that my raising that topic during the meeting had given him the courage to bring it up with his boss in a one-on-one setting. He also created a safe space within his team meetings for parents to connect with one another, share best practices and help each other. By addressing the massive elephant in the room that day, we opened a space to talk about a very important issue. In doing so, we were able to help more working parents after all. To be clear, I still suffered the occasional ugly crying session; however, those were becoming fewer and farther apart. In a global pandemic and economic recession, I considered that a win.

With the coronavirus still raging in the spring of 2020, the world was shaken by another history-making event. The tragic killing of George Floyd impacted society at large and businesses everywhere. The topic of racial discrimination prompted millions across the globe to act, and in the workplace the issue is receiving much deserved and long overdue attention. It would be tone deaf of me to not address that exceptionally important subject in this chapter.

As a white female, I realize I am in the privileged position of never having experienced racism and I would not even pretend to know what it is like to walk a mile in the shoes of my black or racialized colleagues. What I do know is that as a senior leader, I have a responsibility to listen and learn as much as I possibly can, with extreme urgency – and to foster a more inclusive workplace for black employees. In the words of Masai Ujiri, president of the Toronto Raptors: "Your voice matters, especially when you are a leader or an influential figure and especially if you are white. Leaders have to be bold enough to state the obvious and call out racism. The conversation can no longer be avoided because it is hard. We have to have it. Now."[1]

I still have a long way to go in learning and understanding the unique challenges my black colleagues face in their careers. In the meantime, I urge all leaders to engage in this important dialogue and commit to driving meaningful change within your respective organizations. It will take all of us to create truly diverse and inclusive teams and workplaces for all employees regardless of race, gender, age or background. Consider me all-in to contribute in every positive way I can.

---

1   https://www.theglobeandmail.com/opinion/article-masai-ujiri-to-overcome-racism-we-need-to-be-more-than-merely-good/?cmpid=rss&utm_source=dlvr.it&utm_medium=twitter

8

KEEP IT SIMPLE, SISTER

One of the most enjoyable parts of sales leadership is meeting with customers. Over the course of my career I have had the opportunity to attend more than 3,000 client meetings across North America, with the majority taking place on-site at a customer's location.

As a seller, I remember the first time I was asked to bring an executive from my company on a sales call. I was so honored. Two weeks before the meeting, his administrative assistant sent me a lengthy briefing template to prepare. I provided a detailed analysis of the customer's business, including their financials, full bios of everyone with whom we'd be meeting, and a three-year invoice history between our two organizations. The day before the meeting, Mr. Prep and I met. I walked him through all the active projects we were working on with the client and outlined what to expect in the room the following day. The total preparation requirements were time consuming and intense, but I was excited about the value he would bring to the discussion.

The customer meeting itself kicked off normally, with standard introductions and an exchange of business cards. I walked the group through the agenda and we began working our way through the items. Throughout the meeting I kept looking over at Mr. Prep; he was listening intently but saying little. I found this strange, as I had expected him to do much more talking. The customer must have been thinking the same thing and at one point asked Mr. Prep if he had any questions. Straight out of a cheesy sales handbook from 1982, Mr. Prep asked, "What keeps you up at night?" The customer replied casually that he slept soundly and asked if Mr. Prep had any specific questions related to his business or strategic priorities. I was mortified.

On the ride back to the office I felt frustrated. I had spent nearly eight hours preparing briefing information and had such high hopes that Mr. Prep would leverage that information to ask relevant questions that would allow us to accelerate the customer relationship. Instead, he asked a generic question, added little value to the meeting, and ultimately left an undesirable impression with the customer. I spent the next few months quietly praying he would not ask me to take him to more meetings.

As a sales leader, I vowed to do much better. Leading up to a meeting, my approach is simple and does not put an undue burden on sellers. I ask that a seller set up a prep call for the day before the meeting, where I will ask them to answer three simple questions.

1. **What should I know about the customer?** I do my own homework on the customer's business and our mutual business history together, but what specifically should I know walking in? Are they struggling with IT asset management? Are they looking to reduce operational expense this year by 10 percent? Are they skeptical about resellers? These were the nuggets I would not be able to find by doing a Google search or reviewing customer relationship management data.

2. **What is the goal of the meeting?** This sounds incredibly simple, but it is amazing how many times over the years a

seller has struggled to answer this question. Every customer meeting must have a goal. It can be simple – to get them to agree to having us quote on their server project, or to introduce us to a new contact in procurement. Sometimes the goal is simply to secure the *next* meeting with a different department or new contact. Having a clearly defined and desired outcome allows us to work together to achieve it.

3. **What role do you want me to play?** Does the salesperson want me to take the lead? Do they want to split the talking 50-50? Do they want to run point and have me chime in when appropriate? I am comfortable playing any role; I just need to know what it is so we appear organized and in lockstep.

For a straightforward meeting there is no extensive briefing package or rigorous prep session required. A simple prep call that outlines the customer's business challenges, establishes a clear goal and agenda for the meeting and provides an understanding of my role is sufficient. Naturally, for large RFP responses or in-depth strategic presentations to a C-level customer, more preparation is required and we schedule that appropriately.

My approach to meeting debriefs is equally simple. As a rule, I never talk about how the meeting went until I am somewhere private. You never know who is in the elevator or lobby of a building. Once it is safe to do so, I ask the seller three simple questions.

1. **What do you think went well?** A seller's assessment of what they did well in a meeting can tell you quite a bit about their self-awareness. After they provide their thoughts, you can add your perspective, as well as recognizing areas where they really shone. For your A players, it is a great opportunity to help

them build on those strengths in order to be even better next time. It is your Phil Jackson moment.

2. **What do you think we could have done differently?** The best salespeople tend to be the hardest on themselves. They will rattle off a laundry list of things they wished they had said or done differently in a meeting. B and C sellers tend to have a harder time thinking about what they could have done differently. Your opportunity is to provide feedback on areas where your salespeople can improve and help them see their blind spots. Whenever possible, limit your comments to two or three areas of feedback at most; any more than that can be overwhelming. This is also a good time to ask a seller for critical feedback on your own performance in the meeting. Not only does it help improve your skills, it fosters a positive culture where employees can feel comfortable providing feedback in all directions of the organization.

3. **What are the next steps?** The follow-up to a meeting is just as important, if not more important, as the meeting itself. I am a huge proponent of meeting recap emails that clearly document the agreed-upon action items and next steps. It is an effective way to demonstrate to the customer that you were listening during the meeting and it gives them an opportunity to let you know if anything is missing.

From there, the actual follow-up activities are critical. If there is a risk of missing a deadline, proactively letting a customer know and resetting expectations helps to get ahead of any potential escalation. I have always had an email folder called "Pending" where I filed customer items that were not yet complete but were being worked on, by me or someone else. At the end of each day I scanned the folder to determine who needed to get a status update from me.

As a rule, if it had been 48 hours since a customer had last heard from me, I sent a quick note letting them know I hadn't forgotten about them. I told them their item was still being worked on and gave them as accurate an estimated completion time as possible. This small step goes a long way with customers; there is nothing worse than the feeling that something has gone into a black hole. You could be doing all sorts of good things behind the scenes on a customer's behalf, but if you fail to actually let them know that, they might assume you have forgotten or that they are not a priority. Simple and consistent follow-through is what often separates good salespeople and managers from those who are exceptional.

9

ON THE ROAD AGAIN

I have traveled extensively for work purposes, typically between 75 and 100 days every year. A significant portion of my working life has been on the road. This is not easy on me or my family; however, I am blessed to have an extremely hands-on and supportive husband who works hard to make it all possible.

Before every trip, we let our young sons know where Mommy is traveling that week for "work camp" and how many nights she will be away. When I am gone, we do our best to find time for a daily video call so I can catch up with the boys and they can see my face. These tend to have a jarring cinematic quality akin to *The Blair Witch Project*, and most of the conversations with my three-year-old are from the vantage point of looking up his nostrils. But they are special nonetheless.

I have been extremely fortunate to have visited dozens of cities around the world and I've had some unforgettable experiences. But the reality is, most work-related travel is remarkably underwhelming. For me, the most fascinating part about air travel is observing just how much tomato juice gets consumed at 30,000 feet. As a rule, I dislike vegetable-based beverages so I do not partake in this ritual;

however, to this day I have never seen anyone order tomato juice *other* than on an airplane. Do they even sell it at ground level?

Given that travel is often a typical requirement in most sales leadership positions, allow me to share my **Top Five Nuggets** to help guide you on your own journeys through the friendly skies.

1. Whenever possible, carry on your luggage. Nothing good ever comes from checking a bag. I once did a 10-day trip with a carry-on bag and *almost* made it without having to wear a single item twice. Worst case, spending $10 to dry clean an article of clothing at a hotel is still much less costly than spending a significant portion of your life waiting at baggage carousels or risking having your stuff lost or damaged.

2. Nexus and Global Entry are the greatest advancements in air travel since they banned smoking in airplanes. (The concept of a smoking section in a pressurized tube of recycled air never made much sense to begin with.) These time savers are worth every penny and you will not regret the initial investment of about US$50.

3. If you have a small bladder, book an aisle seat. There are few things less glamorous than having to climb awkwardly over another sleeping passenger to use the washroom.

4. Always travel with earplugs. You never know when you will get the hotel room next to that person who watches infomercials at full blast the entire night. While you might appreciate the salesmanship of the gadget-pitching Slap Chop Guy, it is much less intriguing at 4 a.m. when you have an important breakfast meeting in three hours.

5. There is a special place in hell for whomever approved the sale of hard-boiled eggs in airports. I once sat next to a woman on a flight to Dallas who took 45 minutes to eat a boiled egg, while humming along to Celine Dion on her iPod. That was the closest I ever came to experiencing air rage.

In recent years, many industries have gradually moved to the use of video technology to conduct meetings, rather than having their employees travel. The COVID-19 crisis has accelerated this dramatically, pushing virtually the entire corporate world into leveraging video communication as a primary way of meeting. It will be interesting to see what work travel will look like in a post-pandemic era. While I believe nothing will ever replace the value of meeting with customers face to face in their offices or spending time in the field alongside sellers on your team, I do worry about the long-term viability of the tomato juice industry.

10

SUPER SOLVERS, UNITE!

My first couple of months as a new manager were rough. Supervising a large team of salespeople, I constantly felt pulled in different directions and never felt like there were enough hours in the day. I would get home from work feeling exhausted and frustrated. I knew I was spending too much time on things that had little return and they were wearing me down.

I reached out to a company leader I trusted for advice. He told me the key to developing a strong team and creating scale for myself was to stop spending my time on Level 1 and 2 problems. Many managers see their role as Super Solvers of everyone else's issues. They drop everything to play hero whenever anyone needs help and they view their job as that of a fixer. This was the worst thing managers could do for their team, said my adviser, because it creates a culture of learned helplessness. Team members would not develop their own problem-solving skills and the managers would eventually burn themselves out.

It was a wake-up call. He was spot on. Being a Super Solver was exactly the approach I had been taking as a manager. My adviser shared a simple strategy called Five Levels that I embraced immediately and have been leveraging ever since.

THE FIVE LEVELS OF PROBLEM SOLVING

Level 1: I do not know the problem; I do not know the solution.

<u>What this looks like</u>: A seller sprinting into my office, confused, with their hair on fire
<u>What this sounds like</u>: "Something is totally messed up and I have no idea why. Help!"

Level 2: I know the problem, but I do not know the solution.

<u>What this looks like</u>: A seller running into my office with a problem and looking for me to solve it for them
<u>What this sounds like</u>: "My customer is on credit hold; can you fix it?"

Level 3: I know the problem. Here are a couple of solutions I have considered. Which one should I choose?

<u>What this looks like</u>: A seller walking into my office after spending some time thinking about the problem and potential ways to solve it, and asking me to make a decision for them
<u>What this sounds like</u>: "My customer is on credit hold because their account is past due. I'm considering reaching out to my main contact to see if he can get the payments rectified, or going to accounting and asking them to give the customer extended terms. What should I do?"

Level 4: Here is the problem. Here are a few possible fixes. This is the solution I am planning on going with. What do you think?

<u>What this looks like</u>: A seller books time on my calendar. Having carefully considered the situation and possible solutions, they make a recommendation and look to me for support and validation.
<u>What this sounds like</u>: "We shipped my customer a faulty laptop. I have started the return process, but they desperately need new equipment on-site tomorrow. I am likely going to send them a new laptop right away, versus waiting for the return to clear. They have good credit and we have a long history. Are you okay if I do that?"

Level 5: Last week I had this problem, and this is how I solved it. These were the other solutions I considered before making my decision. Your hair looks fabulous.*

<u>What this looks like</u>: A seller debriefing me in our regularly scheduled one-on-one meeting and then going about their day
<u>What this sounds like</u>: "There was a big mix-up last week with my customer's server build that was causing a shipping delay. I called distribution and was able to get it resolved quickly. I considered looking for an alternative off-the-shelf model as I knew it was a rush order. But I decided it was better to take the extra 30 minutes on the phone with the distributor so my customer could remain on their corporate standard model."

Optional*

The goal of the model is simple: coach your salespeople to become Level 4 or 5 problem solvers. At a minimum, get them to Level 3. If a seller comes to you with a Level 1 or 2 problem, have the discipline to send them away and have them come back to you once they get to a higher level. Help them get better at helping themselves.

Implementing the Five Levels of Problem Solving with my team was surprisingly easy. At our next team meeting, I walked everyone through the model and set clear expectations that I would draw a firm line on Level 1 and 2 issues. I was specific in explaining why. The reason was to help them all develop better problem-solving skills and to free up my time to spend more of it working with them on higher impact activities, such as sales calls and coaching sessions.

The concept quickly became a cultural norm on our team and a common language for us. Sellers would come into my office saying, "I could only get this one to a Level 3 and I could really use your help." They became far more self-aware and developed into much better problem solvers. As a manager, it was a game-changer. Suddenly, I had much more time in my day to focus on high-value activities that made a real impact to the team. And as a bonus, I did not burn myself out.

11

499 JOBS

My entire career has been in the technology industry, with most of my experience working for an information technology reseller. Resellers sell IT products and services on behalf of thousands of original equipment manufacturers (OEMs), to thousands of end-user customers. Most OEMs depend heavily on the IT channel to serve as their extended sales force. Resellers and distributors provide OEMs with a significant amount of scale they would not be able to achieve selling directly. For the most part, resellers do not manufacture products of their own. They compete against one another with the value-added support and services they offer. Most importantly, they compete on the customer experience they provide.

Front-line sales teams are critical to a client's experience with a technology provider. At every company where I have worked, the top sellers are rarely the most technical; rather, they are the most resourceful. They become experts on the business priorities of their customers and knowledgeable on the available resources they have, both internally and among OEMs and distributors. Top salespeople organize and align those resources in the most efficient way to help their customers make technology buying decisions, with the ultimate goal of driving business outcomes. Their role is analogous to that of a quarterback on a football team or the conductor of an orchestra.

Relationships and trust are the cornerstone of the technology industry (as they should be in all others) – not only with customers, but within the community itself. In 2012 I met an industry leader and mentor who would have a profound impact on me. Rick Reid was president of a prominent Canadian IT distributor. I had just been promoted to country director for a technology reseller in Canada. While our two companies did a reasonable amount of business together, we had not yet met in person.

I watched Rick work the room at an industry event; he took the time to shake hands with hundreds of attendees. Everyone knew and respected him – he was like the godfather of Canadian IT. Near the end of the evening, Rick approached the table where I was sitting and introduced himself. He congratulated me on my role and said he looked forward to working with me. From then on, Rick made a consistent effort to connect with me and my extended team. He would often ask how his team could better support us and he always made a point of saying thank you for the business and partnership. Rick was gracious and kind, and he treated us as if we were a much bigger player in the market than we were at the time.

Later that year my husband Trevor and I were invited to attend a special industry event in Sonoma, California, co-hosted by Rick and one of our top OEM partners. Each morning my industry peers and I participated in meetings and roundtable discussions while our spouses enjoyed free time. In the afternoons we would all get together for planned social activities. These mainly involved eating and drinking. The official program ended on a Friday night and Trevor and I planned to stay an extra day to enjoy Sonoma, a town in the heart of California wine country. On Saturday morning, we ran into Rick and his wife Lorene in the hotel lobby, along with his colleague Greg and his wife Patricia. The four of them were planning to rent bikes for the day and visit wineries, and Rick asked if Trevor and I would like to join them. We were honored and graciously accepted the invitation.

It was an unforgettable day. The six of us rode together to several wineries and enjoyed incredible wine and food. We shared stories and had many laughs; all four of them made us feel so welcome. It was a wonderful group of people and Rick and Lorene were gracious hosts.

As we were finishing lunch, Rick raised a glass to the group and thanked us all for our company. He then turned to me and said, "I would like to say a special thank you to Cheryl and Trevor for agreeing to join us today, which allows me to expense this lunch." It was a classic Rick Reid line, the first of many I put in my memory vault over the ensuing years.

Rick had a tremendous impact on my career. He taught me the importance of one's brand and reputation in the industry, and the value of building and maintaining strong relationships. I remember calling Rick in 2013 to seek career advice. He said: "I'm going to tell you everything you need to know about the IT channel. There are 500 people in it, and 499 jobs."

Five years later, our young family was moving back to Canada from North Carolina, where we had been living for the previous 12 months. We had been there for my job, which was focused primarily on the U.S. market. Shortly after returning to Canada, I attended an industry forum and got reacquainted with several peers. I thought about Rick's comment from years before and smiled. All the same people were in the room when I came back to Canada, but it was as if half of them had played musical chairs while I was away and ended up in new seats at different companies.

In sales, your reputation and your brand are your biggest assets. However, they can also be your biggest liabilities. Some individuals have risen in the ranks of their sales career using undesirable tactics to get ahead. There are people like this in every profession and every company. I have always believed that in the end, everything comes out in the wash. When they finish their career, how will they be remembered? Likely not fondly, if at all.

Rick Reid taught me to build a positive brand and reputation by demonstrating authenticity and compassion, and prioritizing relationships over everything else. He also taught me that a well-timed one-liner could improve almost any situation.

Whenever I find myself at a career crossroads, I ask myself what Rick would tell me to do. And I wonder if that lunch expense ever got approved.

12

KNOW WHAT?
'BITCHES GET STUFF DONE'

The brilliant Tina Fey has always been one of my heroes. Tina is a talented director, producer, writer, actress – and my future best friend. We have not actually met so she does not yet know this, but I am fully confident she will return my calls and texts any day now and we will hit it off.

Tina declared that "Bitches get stuff done" in an iconic 2008 comedy sketch featured on NBC's *Saturday Night Live*. She was defending Hillary Clinton – often called the B-word by various media outlets – as she contested Barack Obama for the Democratic leadership nomination.

Tina Fey started her comedy career at The Second City, an improvisational comedy group that originated in Chicago. In her best-selling 2011 book *Bossypants*, Tina hilariously explains the Rules of Improv. It occurred to me how applicable the Rules of Improv are to a having successful career in sales leadership.

- **The First Rule of Improv is to say "Yes."** To agree. In an improv performance, if someone starts a scene by saying,

"What a beautiful morning it is on the moon," put on moon boots immediately and start stomping around! By doing so, you have both agreed you are in space and can continue the scene together. In sales leadership, it is also important to start from a place of "Yes" and be open to ideas from your employees, customers, colleagues and managers. By openly welcoming diverse opinions and perspectives at work, your relationships and ultimately your business will grow exponentially.

- **The Second Rule of Improv is the concept of "Yes, And."** Add something that allows the scene to evolve. In the improv moon scene, bust out a birthday cake and invite some stray dogs up to have a space birthday party. What fun! In a sales organization, embracing others' ideas and then building on them sets the stage for continued collaboration and growth.

- **The Third Rule of Improv is to Make Statements.** Doing nothing but asking questions, without ever offering an opinion, can be exhausting. It can zap the energy out of a comedy scene and it puts all the pressure on one person who is forced to come up with all the answers. In sales, the dynamic is similar. While it is important to ask your customers questions so as to understand their business, it is equally critical that you listen to what they are saying and add to the discussion. Otherwise, they will see little value in meeting with you again.

- **Lastly: in improv there are no mistakes, only opportunities.** Whatever direction your partner takes in an improv scene, no matter how absurd, that is the direction you are now going. Embrace it! As a sales leader, never waste a crisis. When a seller screws up with a customer, use it as a coaching opportunity and help them demonstrate to their client how committed they are to resolving the issue promptly and with urgency. If a seller loses a large deal, think of the learnings they can take from the experience to ensure they win the next one. Every negative situation can be leveraged as an opportunity to coach, grow and improve.

At the time of writing this book, I do not have a full-time job. As a result of the COVID-19 crisis, my company restructured the organization and my position was eliminated. Like millions of other Canadians, I found myself unemployed for the first time in my career. The music stopped, and I was not sitting in one of the 499 seats.

While it was unexpected, I have been surprisingly calm about the whole thing. For better or worse, I married the most annoyingly fiscally responsible man on earth, who has been curtailing my otherwise frivolous spending for over a decade. What was irritating for years has suddenly become a blessing, since we are in the fortunate position of not having to panic immediately about making ends meet. Do not get me wrong; the experience of losing my job was not easy to handle. I was initially angry, disappointed and sad. I loved the company I was working for and the incredible team we were building across Canada.

Eventually, I became grateful. I spent nearly eight years of my career with the company and had done seven different jobs during that time. My career accelerated significantly and I made hundreds of connections in the IT channel in Canada and the United States.

I have now been given the opportunity to do something new. I had been thinking about writing for about a year and finally had the time to do it. I am reconnecting with many wonderful people across my extended network while considering my next steps, and using this time to participate in diversity and inclusion events in the IT community. I have much more free time to text with my bestie Tina Fey.

Most importantly, I am spending time at home with my young boys without a trace of guilt. We are building forts, jumping in the swimming pool and playing baseball in the backyard dressed as superheroes. I truly believe the next few months will be the most memorable time of my life, and I hope my children will remember it the same way. But seriously, no more kindergarten Zoom calls. A woman has her limits.

ENDNOTE: UNFINISHED BUSINESS

Most books call this part the "conclusion." I'm not there yet.

While I have learned many valuable lessons in the first 15 years of my sales leadership journey, I hope to chalk up many more in the next chapter of my career, and beyond.

As *The Token Woman* went to press, I started an exciting new role with Amazon Web Services, leading their partner sales organization in Canada. I am confident that I will have many more years of learning, growing and further developing as a sales leader.

Alternatively, I will win the lottery, quit the corporate world and embrace a jet-setting life of decadent luxury and relaxation. Then I will finally read that giant pile of unread business books in my home office!

Who am I kidding? Most likely, I won't.

ACKNOWLEDGMENTS

This book would not have been possible had I not been led by many incredible individuals over the course of my career thus far. My sincerest appreciation to Scott Harper, who took a chance and promoted me to my first sales leadership position when I was 24. The lessons he shared with me early on had an enormous impact on the trajectory of my career and I will be forever grateful.

Thank you to the hundreds of salespeople and leaders who have worked for me over the years. I have learned so much from so many of you. Hopefully, I was not too much of a pain in the ass as your boss.

My sincerest thanks to Mary Jo Cartwright for her editing support and for helping me tell the stories that have been circulating in my brain for the last few years.

Thank you to Dina Zuchkan, who saw something in an outspoken teenager in her grade 10 drama class and introduced me to the world of improv comedy. My thanks for many years of teaching, friendship, and mutual distrust of cats.

To the past and present board members and key contributors of WiSH (Women in SHI): thank you for having the vision to create a more diverse and inclusive workforce and for asking me to be a part of the mission. A special shout-out to Shannon Sigmon, Melissa

Humble and Valerie Henderson. I am a better leader and person for having had the opportunity to work alongside the three of you for many years.

To my parents, John Stookes, Sharon Neely and late stepdad Bob Neely – who affectionately referred to me as his "rotten child" for more than two decades. I would not be the person I am today without the encouragement and unconditional love of my amazing parents.

Finally, to my husband Trevor and sons Alexander and Cameron. Thank you for your endless love and support, and for usually remembering to put pants back on when I arrive home from work trips. Thank you for pretending not to hate it when I sing. You three are my whole world and I love you very much. But seriously, please put on pants.

CPSIA information can be obtained
at www.ICGtesting.com
Printed in the USA
BVHW030816021120
592246BV00005B/8